TAILS from History

A Sea Otter to the Rescue

By **Thea Feldman**
Illustrated by **Rachel Sanson**

Ready-to-Read

Simon Spotlight

New York London Toronto Sydney New Delhi

SIMON SPOTLIGHT
An imprint of Simon & Schuster Children's Publishing Division
1230 Avenue of the Americas, New York, New York 10020
This Simon Spotlight edition June 2019
Text copyright © 2019 by Simon & Schuster, Inc.
Illustrations copyright © 2019 by Rachel Sanson

For information about special discounts for bulk purchases, please contact Simon & Schuster Special
Sales at 1-866-506-1949 or business@simonandschuster.com.
Manufactured in the United States of America 0519 LAK
10 9 8 7 6 5 4 3 2 1
Library of Congress Cataloging-in-Publication Data
Names: Feldman, Thea, author. | Sanson, Rachel, illustrator.
Title: A sea otter to the rescue / by Thea Feldman ; illustrated by Rachel Sanson.
Description: Simon Spotlight edition. | New York : Simon Spotlight, 2019. | Series: Tails from history |
Audience: Age 5–7.
Identifiers: LCCN 2018043072 | ISBN 9781534443389 (hardcover) | ISBN 9781534443372 (paperback) |
ISBN 9781534443396 (eBook)
Subjects: LCSH: Sea otter—California—Monterey Bay—Biography—Juvenile literature.
Classification: LCC QL795.O8 F45 2019 | DDC 599.769/50979476—dc23
LC record available at https://lccn.loc.gov/2018043072

It was a summer day in 2001.
There was a new sea otter
at an aquarium in California.

The sea otter's name was Toola.
Toola was a grown-up sea otter—
about five years old.
She was sick because of cat litter
that had been dumped into the ocean.
Toola needed medicine every day
to stay healthy.

The aquarium rescues sick sea otters
because they are endangered
(say: en-DANE-jurd).
That means they are at risk
of disappearing forever.
There are only about three thousand
wild sea otters living in California.

The aquarium took good care
of Toola.
She quickly settled into
her new home.
She liked to make the staff
chase her in the water.

Soon after, a rescued baby sea otter
was brought into the aquarium.
A baby sea otter is called a pup.

This pup was an orphan.
No one knew what had happened
to his mother.

He was only two weeks old.
That is much too young
for a pup to be on his own.

In the past,
some of the aquarium staff
had raised sea otters.
The humans had become parents
for the orphaned pups.

When the pups were ready
to return to the ocean,
the staff put tags
on the pups' flippers.
This way, the aquarium could track
the otters in the wild.

However, very few of these sea otters lived long in the wild.
Maybe it was because they had spent too much time with humans.

This time, the staff had an idea. What if they gave the new orphaned pup to Toola? She was old enough to be a mother.

No one knew what would
happen if they paired a pup
with another sea otter.
Would Toola raise the pup
as her own?

The pup floated on his back.
He didn't know how to swim.
Toola swam up to him.
She reached toward the pup
with her front paws.

Then she pulled him onto her chest,
just like any mother otter would do.
Toola had adopted the pup!

Toola was a good mother.
She opened clamshells
and shared them with the pup.

When the pup was ready,
Toola taught him how to swim.
She pulled him along in the water
and encouraged him
to use his flippers.

She taught him how to dive, too.
Sea otters have to dive
to find their food.
They like to eat shellfish,
such as clams and crabs,
that live on the ocean floor.

Toola showed the pup
how to open a hard shell.
She put a rock on her chest.
Then she hit the shell against
the rock until the shell cracked!

She even taught the pup
how to make sure a crab
would not pinch his nose!

A sea otter's fur keeps it warm
and dry in the water.
The fur must always stay clean,
so Toola spent many hours every day
cleaning the pup's fur.

Then Toola showed him
how to groom his fur.
She rubbed and licked her own fur.
She turned over and over
in the water.

When the pup was about
six months old, he was ready
to return to the ocean.
The staff tracked the pup
with a tag. They watched him
grow up in the wild and
have many pups of his own!

Toola had taught the pup
to be a great sea otter!
She had done what no sea otter
at the aquarium had done before.

Toola stayed at the aquarium
to continue taking her medicine.
She raised twelve more pups.
She went from being rescued
by the aquarium staff
to rescuing other sea otters!

There are now many sea otters
who raise orphaned pups
at the aquarium.

A young boy heard about Toola.
His dad was a lawmaker
in California. He asked his dad
to write a law to protect sea otters.
The law passed in 2006.
It allows people to donate money
to the endangered sea otters.

People have donated more than
three million dollars,
thanks to Toola!

The law helps scientists
who study sea otters.
This way, the scientists can learn
how to protect them in the wild.

Toola lived to be fifteen or sixteen years old. She was always busy raising pups or just having fun. Toola had no idea she was the most important sea otter in the aquarium's history!

· Facts about Sea Otters ·

- Toola was a southern sea otter. They live along the coast of California.
- Sea otters are the largest members of the weasel family.
- Sea otters can hold their breath for up to five minutes.
- Sea otters sleep while floating on their backs.
- Humans have about a hundred thousand hairs on their heads. Sea otters can have up to one million hairs per square inch. That is the most fur per square inch of any animal!

· How You Can Help Sea Otters ·

- Throw away your trash properly. Litter can pollute the ocean.
- Write to your lawmakers and ask them to help protect sea otters and other marine life.
- If you ever see a sea otter, keep your distance. They may be cute, but touching them is unsafe for the otter and for you.
- If you have a pet cat, don't flush the cat litter down the drain. Cat litter contains bacteria that makes sea otters sick.
- Spread the word about sea otters. Tell your family and friends how they can help too!